THE HUMAN FACE

T0290388

Also by Iain Crichton Smith *from* Carcanet

A Life
Ends and Beginnings
Collected Poems
Selected Poems
Selected Stories

Iain Crichton Smith

THE HUMAN FACE

CARCANET

First published in 1996 by
Carcanet Press Limited
402-406 Corn Exchange Buildings
Manchester M4 3BY

A CIP catalogue record for this book
is available from the British Library
ISBN 1 85754 251 7

The publisher acknowledges financial assistance
from the Arts Council of England

Set in 10 pt Joanna by Bryan Williamson, Frome
Printed and bound in England by SRP Ltd, Exeter

Man's inhumanity to man
makes countless thousands mourn.

O wad some Power the giftie gie us
to see oursels as ithers see us!
It wad frae mony a blunder free us
        an' foolish notion:
What airs in dress and gait wad lea'e us,
        an' even devotion!

Robert Burns

That ethnic differences should
lead men into a darkling wood
stained with an internecine blood
    is to be mourned
when there is much beatitude
    within our bourne.

That dogmas snap at heel and head
with bitter teeth: and that deep red
dresses the bride who might have wed
    is cruel fact:
these are the tracks of those who fled
    in cataracts

of children, women. Neighbours once
they were united in the dance
of a diurnal circumstance
    of grief and joy:
but now some raise obsessive guns
    at girl and boy.

As if at Hallowe'en they wear
patches of ancestry and dour
dogmas composed from out the air
    (for Nature isn't,
O seasonal Nature's not aware
    of more than present).

Ceilidhs you held in common halls,
you had luxurious carnivals,
but now we see such crimson palls
    as scorch the gaze:
there leap across your local walls
    blood-red ideas

of kin and creed, to smash a door.
Members of an élitist corps
you tear at the colourful décor
        that men must build
to identify that they are here,
        by self beguiled.

Nature unconsciously swells
to green and red: and it compels
even human buildings to its rules,
        a passionate queen
of weeds and lilies and bluebells,
        a rage of green.

But conscious man will kill and smash
frail secret envelopes of the flesh –
hack at beard and at moustache –
        because he's armed
with ideas made of patchy trash
        that grief's confirmed,

or loneliness or heritage,
or a new-learned unfocused rage.
O he's a vulture in a cage
        that has been shaped
by others than himself – typed page
        from manuscript.

Anthologies are justified
from gods and creeds to let men ride
on tall infernal horses. Pride
        plays lovely flutes.
Who leads this troop but Homicide
        with shining boots?

Their heavenly uniform is blue,
and complex theories tattooed
are pictures of a large and crude
    comic-strip idea.
Green nature did not once imbue
    such vicious fear,

but is composed of trees and stones,
and not these merciless monotones.
Melodious birds play different tunes
    at night or day –
my lovely throstles, larks and wrens,
    multi-voiced play!

Christians, Moslems and Hindus
have built a shelter from bad news
from creeds from which they pick and choose
    lest they should die
alone in tenement or mews
    beneath a sky

unscripted by a higher hand.
They build a pure Utopian land
where there is 'neither rain nor wind
    nor mist nor snow'
from which they gaze on the unplanned
    chaos below.

I've heard one say a Catholic
is a close acquaintance of Old Nick,
a Fenian bastard fit for brick
    or knife or bullet.
The Pope wears green, a politic
    fat Pontius Pilate.

Across the now-anointed Boyne
there rides a horse – O heaven-born.
Truth sparkles from its saddle horn,
        O brightly blue,
and a flag is raised to firmly burn
        for the favoured few.

Of course Mohommedan and Sikh,
The Turk and the 'perfidious Greek',
the Jew and his 'usurious clique'
        are also shaped
to dwell in that demonic reek,
        by the inept.

The jester wore his tunic once
in double colour: he would prance
and joke for his empurpled prince
        at laden table.
He saved himself by shifty stance,
        sparkling, unstable.

But those who wear idea's hues,
tunics of yellow, red or blue,
endorse one colour and enthuse
        about its virtues.
O always heaven's precious news
        must come in courteous

monolingual monochrome.
For God when He is at home
and writing drama, prose, or poem
        has a one-hued ribbon.
He is imperialist as Rome
        was before Gibbon.

One only colour and décor
is what God loves. That is His gloire.
Flags constitute his long histoire
    and they are ours.
Let spring burst richly by the Loire
    with *single* flowers.

Flags wave above the random stones,
are winding sheets above men's bones:
because of them we hear the moans
    of dying flesh,
while knifing geriatric crones
    bitterly slash.

Over the ground in green and red
above the pale anonymous dead
from whom their riotous blood has bled
    the flags make sail.
Whereto, we ask. To lively trade
    or credal jail?

Ideas clash as soldiers toil
in naïve energy to foil
their enemies' imperial style
    backed by the critics.
There is a vicious bloody boil
    of different ethics.

Naïve soldier, you may be just
fighting your own interest
and the flag you capture with hot wrist
    may be your own,
and the knife that twists inside your breast
    made of your bone.

Flags that cast shadows on the ground
are making 'natural' each wound
that reddens green. O they have crowned
    that ort of soil
as if quite artlessly they've found
    their own best style.

Life's various and bright discourses
are simplified by men and horses
who stamp their dialects on courses,
    brutal, inhuman,
and black sun-sparkling winding hearses
    crush 'foreign' women.

Maidens and matrons now are whores
and titled so among these flowers –
malignant loose caricatures
    of 'Mary Mother'
whose gaze 'invariant and pure'
    is clear as water.

O there are styles of war as well –
erasures, changes, the pell-mell
inspiring charges. And there swell,
    like shadows, books.
Bibles, like eagles, soar and fall
    down on Karl Marx.

Scholars in closets sharpen swords
and beards point down like midnight swords
and treatises from sheltered cowards
    conjure red fields
on which men fall like packs of cards
    to the spade's rich yield.

Behind the armies always are
casuists unfitted for a war
who gloss their idiot, bizarre,
        inhuman, theses,
and say that a unique and brilliant star
        confirms excesses.

The pen behind the legions carves
bodies and trenches: O it serves
to straighten life's most generous curves
        and will not shift
though contradictory reserves
        to right and left

mock margins of the sacred page.
The sentences of righteous rage
are ornamented with their sage
        footnotes from heaven.
Men of a certain lineage
        can't be forgiven.

So ministers with axes hack
from their demented zodiac
at the unholy bric-a-brac
        of men and women,
the rubbish that bestrews the track
        of the inhuman.

And soldier, priest, together are
the Gemini of that baleful star
which shines so swartly from the far
        realms of idea
on tattered orphans set on fire
        for Obadiah

or some such prophet.
                    Words withdraw
from that long oceanic roar
which resonates along the shore
      of our fierce times.
But someone needs the safe décor
      of human rhymes.

And so the winding German train
will snake its way among the green
pastoral valley to an insane
      and ordered camp,
while gas, like rumour, hisses in
      rooms where the lamp

of Handel once or Kant or Brahms
shone from a day of lovely calms.
What charms you had, and now what arms
      are thin as sticks.
Hidden among the cherry farms
      what rifle clicks?

And Beethoven with craggy head
lowers on this banquet of the dead,
and Mozart sparkles in the pride
      of a supreme
genius seemingly self-taught,
      a brilliant stream.

And others too like Hölderlin
Heine, Goethe, Thomas Mann,
gaze down with horror as that train
      winds through a wood
which once was vernal now insane,
      a world of blood,

where leaves of spring convert to leaves
inscribed with gibberish, false beliefs.
Wasp-waisted gauleiters conceive
    themselves as gods,
pure as the desert. Truth's engraved
    on their tall swords.

My dearest poets, artists, who
never use poems to pursue
the helpless or the ill-to-do
    or write, 'I know
the meaning of the world I view –
    it is just so.

'And if you don't believe my rhyme
I'll be the policeman, you the crime.
Why should you interrupt my chime
    with frivolous you.
For surely I'm the paradigm
    you must construe.

'And you are nothing, only fit
for adverb in my manuscript:
to march to metre, be upright
    for a page or two.
You're less than a word in my great ode,
    so huge and new.'

O if such or such were said
how could we flower beside the dead
Shakespeare and Wordsworth at their trade
    on this vast globe
of various green and blue and red
    expansive hubbub?

To kill the other you must make
on our image-conscious and fake
seething screen, him sordid rake
    and corrupt foe,
a devilish construction, mage
    of malign glow.

His children also must be set
as demons from a seething pit
of hairy fetor and of sweat,
    of pagan sex.
Infants who gaze through innocent light
    envisage wrecks

of your society and home.
O they are not a lyric poem
which needs just here and there a comb,
    but treacherous words
which on pretence of play and rhyme
    are vicious swords.

So children too are spitted, shot,
burnt, buffeted, to small bones brought.
Let famine gnaw them till they rot
    in tiny graves,
and let the little wooden cot
    swing in the gales

of terror, hunger, and deceit.
Betray your neighbour, lie and cheat.
O he has such vast conceit,
    so must be demon
sinful, proud, and absolute,
    surely inhuman.

Even the way he runs his mower,
the green paint which adorns his door,
these show him even in décor
    as one of THEM.
The very suit he chose to wear
    is made of flame.

The way he speaks, the way he walks,
the shape and glamour of his socks,
these all show him as the fox
    the hound must kill.
The scent of him abhors! The shock
    of his different style!

So, dogma, bring me help in this
correct and pure analysis.
His Mrs also and his Miss
    are devilish odd.
Help me from monotheistic skies,
    unchanging God!

Eternal being just the same
in brilliant sunshine or in storm
who knows the everlasting aim
    for all believers,
even the blinded and the lame,
    and high achievers.

Even the legless, the one-eyed,
the bridegroom who has lost his bride,
the obedient and the parricide
    and the asthmatic.
All his constituents abide
    by the programmatic

menu served from His high skies.
O let Him rightly terrorise
those stylists who will advertise
    their own new suits.
O let Him puncture their devised
    'safe' parachutes.

Look how He teased old Abraham
by almost killing his pet lamb
though He did substitute a ram
    at the last minute.
It was a grand tremendous game
    played in the finite

mountains and the valleys. So
He'd cut a tribe of Gentiles low
and relish much to hear Jews blow
    triumphant horns
as new generations do
    with space-age planes.

O God, who chose one not the other
and has set brother against brother
as Cain and Abel (meat, and weather-
    exalted barley.
Farmer and hunter sway together
    in hurly burly).

Murder and cheating are to You
no rending of that seamless blue
which always looks so fresh and new
    even when jets
whiz faster than the Dove once flew
    across the wet

ocean, with greenery in its mouth,
and Noah knew that God's great wrath
had dwindled to a sunny path
    across the wave
and a rainbow, shimmering, was worth
    a million graves:

bow of colour in the sky,
a brilliant phantom archery,
diaphonous arc, God's sorcery
    to forgive the dead
whose mouths were gagged with brine. They lie
    head by drenched head,

the fruit of salt, the figs of green
waters now pleasant and serene.
O what a docile tranquil scene
    from such a storm
as makes the rainbow lurid crayon,
    or wriggling worm.

In such does cruelty begin,
in tyranny its origin,
in the single eye that burns the brine
    and so permits
neighbourly foe on foe to dine
    as at the Ritz

when plate on plate is red with gore
and hoods appearing at the door
spray virgin tablecloths.
                Décor
    of instant roses
adorns the breasts of those who poured
    wine for their spouses.

And even now the coffined dead
are swept by gunfire, the graveyard
is target for the sniper's hard
    and stately eye.
The mourners flee from side to side
    and scream and cry

as bullets bounce from inscribed stone
and track the name of Sean or John
or Serbian or Croatian
    husband or wife –
even the sleeping derelict bone
    no longer safe,

but stitched, unstitched, by lead and fire
as Death types out his literature,
one-sided, terrible, bizarre,
    of local red.
Among the mourners, here is Mars
    at his best trade.

So even 'ceremony's drowned'
as Yeats foretold, as guns resound
and even the 'centre cannot hold'
    but shrapnel breaks
in all directions.
               Gyres unfold
    from local sects.

Unjust imperialism cracks
and breeds the local blood-red axe.
Great rusty doors creak open. Wrecked
    machines appear.
Behind once loved ideals, packs
    of demons wear

hypocrisies of words and dress.
Among the ruined webs they blessed
with flags and texts, they now egress
        into stunning light.
What cobwebs wave behind the gloss
        of style and rite!

where selfish pelf and greed have seethed
behind the rusty door, enwreathed
with bouquets, sermons, all bequeathed
        by geriatric
fur-clad minds which could hardly breathe
        in our electric

century. How grey the east
compared with our seeming-prosperous west
where all is marketable excess,
        even death itself,
and men may pick their dearest vice
        straight from the shelf.

Grey sparseness, or the purple robe
in our delirious hubbub –
empire directs its brilliant strobe
        one way or other.
Behind the curtain, similar rogues
        confront each other,

avaricious grazers on the toil
which the plebs contribute. O, their oil
fills tanks and planes to keep a style
        firmly in place,
while others play their flutes and spoil
        our common days.

The rusty door breaks open. Tragic
how it was all a sort of magic
trick, played against all logic:
        gold was just lead,
and what seemed firmly theologic
        old webs instead.

Old broken cars, and not Rolls Royces,
human and not predestined voices,
bad poems and not gold-plated verses
        sent from above,
the hand that waved from travelling hearses
        wore a mailed glove.

And behind that desolate grey scene
travelled a shining limousine
reserved for autocrat, monseign-
        eur or dictator.
The jails are where the best convene
        to vanish later

from this dull grey and monochrome
unchanging weather, just like Rome
or other empire plebs may roam
        their ill-lit streets
but elaborate music fills the dome
        with old forged notes

to commemorate victories, space-races,
pomp that's been squeezed from pallid faces
who blinded by paralysis
        of glory bled
in statisticians' embraces –
        the fatal pride

of paper, propaganda, graph.
False figures climb like planes. They strafe
the foe with braggadocio, guff,
        till he in turn
grows monstrous frog, or tall giraffe,
        peering, to learn

the secrets of the golden door
(which really is rusty, desolate, poor).
How could a demon laugh out more
        than at this sport,
the telescope that hour by hour
        tracks famished fort,

rusty machinery, starving plebs,
the iron armoury, the strobes
that rainbow these poor tattered tribes
        and failing fields.
Above the rags a glowing robe,
        metallic shield.

Oh, how not mourn what we've become!
The collapse of an imperium
grown as arthritic as old Rome
        breeds miniature selves!
New-whelped beasts are adult grown
        to vicious wolves,

snapping and biting from their dens.
Mountains resound to rusty guns.
A sniper fires and someone runs
        across a road.
And who is that pointing his lens?
        O is it God,

a single Being. None but He
you worship in your uniform, gay
in your excessive ecstasy
    of lethal red.
The wine you drink even as you pray
    is human blood,

a Yugoslavian concoction,
an Irish fion, of fine conviction,
a divine Somalian confection
    a connoisseur
has woven out of moral fiction
    and ethnic gloire.

O do not drink. That twisted face
contorted by your ethics is
your human brother, not a prize
    for your revolver.
See how his scared uncertain eyes
    fearfully waver.

See him, see him, as he is,
conspicuous and piteous,
not any better any worse
    than you yourself.
His throat, in cold, will become hoarse,
    his heart feel grief.

He has his mortgage or his rent,
his photos tell of a descent
as poor as yours. A regiment
    summoned to colours
through lies and fogs, this man who went
    to appalling horrors,

just like yourself, your sad confrère
who has his place on this drenched terre
who is to father, mother, chèr
     as you to yours.
Who wants to lie in mud or stour
     for crows to pierce?

Mirror, mirror, he is you
though clad in that transcendent blue,
he feels the fever and the flu
     of human pains.
He's pinched by a similar holed shoe
     which lets in rains.

Who wants to feel the bullet's weight
propel him backwards from the light,
the sunny pathos that ignites
     both leaf and bush?
Who wishes flies to play and bite
     eye or moustache?

Who wishes to be dead and stark
under the brave delirious lark
or sail the melancholic barque
     down the black Styx,
or hear the dog of Hades bark
     from ebony rocks?

Who'd rather not on Saturday
watch the football or TV
or see his little children play
     with runny noses?
These are preferable to the grey
     of death's hypnosis.

We grow among untitled stones
but then the green or blue condones
the kicks and sticks and deaths and groans
    we inflict on others.
Halleluiah to these monotones,
    sing opposite brothers.

Under this warranty of death
we hold our briefly-rented breath.
Why therefore knock your brother's teeth
    deep down his throat?
And why lay an explosive wreath
    at the grave's mouth.

Perfidious Dogma, lethal flag,
intolerant of dialogue,
for you, red murder is the vogue
    both night and day:
inciting horror and intrigue
    and paranoia.

Your human skin is marbly grown,
a smooth impermeable shine,
impenetrable and divine,
    immune to sorrow.
Yesterday is where you're in.
    What of tomorrow?

We need our yesterdays, it's true.
For we're not animals in a zoo,
and backward we can cast our view
    on prospects drear
or sometimes idyllic. Often blue
    our summers were.

And depthless Fascism compiles
superficial anthologies of ills,
the naked brutal instant will,
        the polished pistol,
infernal technologies of skill
        and hearts of crystal.

But living in the past is worse
than travelling in a constant hearse.
Along the same old rutted course
        and ancient paths
both blue and green, rides the white horse
        of psychopaths

who see, not present, but the past
through icy sights. The trigger's pressed
and a breathing victim stands aghast
        to be so taken
for someone opinionated, dressed
        in antique fashion.

Into an earlier century fires
the sniper with the boiling eyes.
Serb or Croatian expires
        in another age.
You may find the cause in literature's
        preceding page.

Antiquities leap out as new
and what once was is what you do.
An ancient manuscript gives the clue
        to present slaughter.
A cliché furnishes the cue
        to destroy a culture.

Deep, deep, in the archaeology
of mind and psyche children cry
and wounded men and women sigh
        and houses fall,
and living generations die
        so to fulfil

prophecies cast by vicious egoes,
nervous Macbeths or blunt Iagos,
the Lutheran terrors and imagos
        of which Auden wrote,
and which produced the tall viragos
        at Belsen's court.

In winter you've seen frozen grass
sparkling and brilliant as glass
but what if it always was
        such blinding crystal,
surely we'd have found perverse
        those pentecostal

frigid and rigid stalactites
sharp and distinct in uniform light
another age had cast about
        our mortal traces.
Surely we'd rather trail our feet
        through living grasses,

than from these icy fields project
a meagre obsessive intellect
and slowly carefully construct
        our chilly fences
against old legions, now defunct,
        and circumstances

decayed and waste in earlier deaths
arrayed and dressed in earlier clothes
made long ago for earlier moths
        to bite great holes in.
A spectral Nelson still obsessed
        with spectral Napoleon,

or England still with Joan of Arc,
or the rose of Lancaster with York,
or mailed Crusader still with Turk,
        or Gaul with Roman,
or seagreen Robespierre with Burke,
        Saxon with Norman.

O let us see men as they are,
not flagged and wigged in a bizarre
museum fitted out for war
        by puppeteers,
who cannot love our common star
        days, weeks, or years

in its routine pathos and allure,
but need the panoply of war,
its exciting eloquence and glamour
        and bloody steel
to copy out their portraiture
        and make them real.

Study the past. O, yes, we should,
to maintain our egoes in the flood
of light which pours around us, roads
        of difficult ethics.
But to live in the past is merely food
        for psychopathics,

fixed in their unchanging station
eternal in the God they fashion
to adorn their rifles and their motion
    in hoods and masks
and make destruction their profession
    and major task,

gangsters who burst through innocent rooms
in death's cold black. Boom boom boom boom
they bring their 'brave delirium'
    to cure by fire
deviants from the imperium
    their 'souls' desire.

See how their vague abstractions cloud
each pitiful and leaking shroud.
It is not they, no, it is God
    who exacts His justice,
or it might be Marx, it might be Laud,
    or cold Augustus,

or, better, 'honour', 'order', 'gloire',
'democracy' or 'a just war',
'the Soul of Developing Histoire'
    which is determined;
the 'State', the 'Government', austere
    and hard as diamond.

Windy abstractions fill the day
and blow individuals away
and real faces mist and sway
    in Honour's fog,
in one imperious idea
    and monologue.

And death becomes a friendly fire.
Against that sharp and fatal wire
for King and Country you expire
    while red-faced majors
threaten and posture in the mire
    behind their soldiers.

And clerics urge their armies on.
Their bibles like the rifles burn.
Is that an angel or a plane?
    Cloud of unknowing,
theology makes that man's brain
    as red as rowan.

It's a cartoon of windy nouns.
Fraternity will now announce
grey smoke and cannonade of guns –
    Equality
will lay more bodies on the ground
    in pale-faced Gravity.

Above the battlefield there rises
'Beloved Fatherland in a Crisis',
'A patient people exercises
    its General Will'
or 'I will hammer up my thesis
    for good or ill.'

Abstractions eat the concrete, as
prehistoric monsters race
through swampy plains with gaping jaws
    and scaly torsos,
with malice sparkling from their eyes
    as from First Causes.

Fogs of abstractions fight above
our good plain earth, and splenitive
ambitious chefs cut out and carve
        demonic courses
of human flesh obscenely served,
        and even horses.

How is it that we cannot *see,*
instead of false infinity,
the shattered face, the fractured knee,
        the empty socket,
the pilot targetting that tree,
        that whizzing rocket.

O it's not heaven that is divine
but this dear landscape we define
by local habitation, sign
        of stone and valley
which should not hear the eerie whine
        of a reveille.

Why should we let some preaching zealot
avid to resurrect the helot,
crow like a cockerel, a prelate
        cameras pan on.
O what is truth, said jesting Pilate.
        Canon or cannon?

That life is dicey, we may grant.
Accidents, disease, haunt
even sunny days, and we descant
        on their first causes.
What's given is not what we want.
        We suffer losses,

griefs, terrors, loneliness, despair.
Some will prosper, some will wear
cast offs, rags. And some, prepared,
      will feel the lightning
whiz across their head and hair,
         unexpected, frightening.

And so they pray that these quite neutral
days, seemingly so brutal,
will favourably shine on mortal
      but blessed bones.
'Let me at least be saved. I'll settle
      my debt with hymns.'

It's fear proposes their religion.
It's fear that fires them with conviction.
It's fear that makes them seek prediction
      by horoscope
or see God in perpetual action
      with telescope.

And so they build their ceremonial
chapels, and make others menial.
Their voices rise, entranced, hymeneal,
      to God invisible.
The ego, humble and subliminal,
      will then make possible

statements of stunning central verve.
'I believed, was saved,
                        Though others starve
or Scuds or similar rockets curve
      on other nations
Yet You were pleased to make them swerve
      their fixed formations

'from me, and so I bless you, God.
I do not find it strange or odd
that I be saved while others died
    in Your vast furnace.
Surely it's because I prayed
    in ceremonious

'style as was taught me.
                    Alcoholic
I blundered through your fine idyllic
world, was vitriolic
    to wife and children,
but later learnt the apostolic
    forgiving syndrome.

'And so I march with gun or flute
sparkling in a sparkling light,
a servant of the single God
    who saved my soul.
Though others starved or drowned or died
    I yet was whole.'

And strict Mohammedan, or Hindu,
Baptist, Methodist, or Jew,
will say the same, and all construe
    their Holy Book
as entitling them to be first in queue
    for God to pick.

And so it is that tiny sects
on windy islands, derelict,
on margins of the world expect
    God's full attention.
And all the ships untimely wrecked?
    Why, God's intention.

Whatever happens is divine,
and all events are His design,
who turned the water into wine
    or raised the dead.
The holocaust was just a sign
    hung out by God.

And so it's He who let a Führer
ideally contemplate a purer
German heaven: by means of terror
    disinfect a state
to blue-eyed, blonde-haired and superior
    children of light.

And so the trains by His permission
slide with their evil undulation
through landscapes neutral of expression
    to tranquil stations
where Death in sparkling gloves and dress
    is calmly waiting.

And devout students of the Torah
rub their eyes and find tomorrow
and human joy and human sorrow
    have disappeared
with cap and Bible and bravura
    of well-cropped beard.

History's fond of such erasures,
a sort of brutal Occam's razor
which opens surgical sharp fissures
    in time's rough stuff.
As in a theatre of pleasures,
    they're there, then puff!

they vanish and a blank remains.
Where once they acted an intense
role in the play called Circumstance
        and brought the house down
they've now become a dissonance
        that needs adjusting.

superfluous to the New Idea
and the assembly line of Fear
which runs on blood and bones, austere
        shining machine
the heavens project from there to here
        as guillotine.

A Danton or a Trotsky kicks
briefly against History's pricks
or down the unforgiving Styx
        a Robespierre
drifts in his lawyer's orthodox
        tight-buttoned gear.

The editor orders. 'This must go.'
and runs his red pen through the flow
of the unending to and fro;
        and this is right
according to the fixed tableau
        of God's own thought.

Whatever is is right. This is
the conservative hypothesis
it's sin to question or to quiz.
        Viz, you may say
a dinner at Auschwitz or the Ritz
        is equal fare.

Why therefore have a God at all,
if what happens is the real,
if Evil or Good is what befalls:
        and what occurs
is sign of God's eternal will,
        better or worse.

As well might say, That rainbow isn't
God's advertisement in the present
flood of the temporary, evanescent,
        subsiding waters
but simply a rainbow, fluorescent
        painting in nature's

endlessly inventive art,
and changing gallery, a sort
of radiance, and not purport
        of marvellous gesture
dramatically to subvert
        an earlier posture.

If what happens is God's intent
if every happening is what's meant
then it need not be God's lineament
        that shines from high
to justify each good event
        or devilry.

If Fact and God are just the same
why should a Jewish scholar aim
his monocle at the world's frame
        to find God there –
the holocaust also and its shame
        imprinted on air.

And why did God permit those trains
to travel so easily from towns
and ghettoes where His Chosen ones
        huddled in fright.
Why did he not send thunderstorms
        or gelignite

or plagues of frogs as He did once
to mulish Pharaoh, or flies to munch
himself, his servants, and his lunch,
        while silent Moses
unpractised in smooth eloquence
        led out his forces.

O did You will that those sad shoes
of the children of your Chosen Jews
should be gathered now in blank disuse
        in that Museum's
narration of horrific news
        in Jerusalem,

while nevertheless not guns but stones
are hurled by Palestinians
as if imitating David's stance
        before Goliath.
What swart and baleful planet shines
        in Nazareth.

O history turns about, about,
in all its fascinating fact
nor is it God who thus inflicts
        war on new war.
Nor is it God who contemplates
        his errant, bizarre

planet which red 'sin' disfigures.
Why should rabbinical Jew be staggered
while examining with nocturnal ardour
    mediaeval texts,
or a Greek urge for perfect order
    make circles best

when really the orbits were elliptic
which would have solved the intricate cryptic
Ptolemaian convoluted
    shapeless huddle,
a crazy hypothesis created,
    mind-boggling muddle.

How many madmen used divine
texts to inflict their asinine
and poisonous creeds on yours and mine
    and swell their egoes
like balloons above the flowing Rhine
    or luminous logos

of a new sorcery or sect.
'Save your soul. Join the Elect.'
Here is the enemy who wrecked
    your legitimate aims.
It is quite easy to detect
    their devilish names.

Leave family and friends and come.
Follow the music of our drum.
How easily you will become
    handsome, and free
from puzzlement, delirium,
    day's misery.

Inflict on others what you bore.
Now you'll find what pain is for.
Destroy the demons, learn to pour
        hot fires among them,
or sit them in an iron chair
        and quite untongue them.

And as you torture them your brow
becomes serene again. They bow
and jerk as fiddlers do
        in your new music
of violins or of violence. So,
        a healthy physic

to keep you happy, puzzle-free!
Exaggerated energy
will flow through head and breast and knee
        and flush you clean.
O all that harsh brutality
        leaves you serene,

godlike. Crush those tiny skulls.
Use your best inventive skills
to perpetrate ingenious styles
        of human torture.
You have a cool and clinical pulse
        as God's good creature.

Ambassador of terror, bring
your doctor's knowledge to this ring
and as you probe serenely, sing
        a psalm or hymn,
while all around you blithely sing
        the seraphim

smelling of chloroform and soap,
cocktail of dettol and cheap dope,
God with his tranquil telescope
    looks from the skies.
Work, as you claim, with social hope
    and expertise.

Why don't you cut their 'evil' out?
It may reside in eye or throat.
It may be that small 'damnèd spot'
    or in the thorax
it may be hiding from the light.
    Scourge it with borax!

This hospital is for demonic
cleansing, or for eugenic
experiments. The moronic
    can expect no mercy
and yet you also are Hellenic,
    civilised, easy

raconteur, anaesthetist.
See how pale your hand and wrist.
Your jewelled watchlike 'soul's' good taste
    is systematic.
You are an exquisite analyst
    of the problematic.

O you may genially fix
machinery as full of tricks
as an articulate sonnet is
    but less fictitious,
for it explodes – and will not miss –
    its light conspicuous.

It changes facts to what you wish,
Billy or James, all those judic-
ious dead who, in emerald, fished
    those ancient streams:
or those whose portraits are enmeshed
    in Serbian streams.

Tell me, tell me, how it is
that modern rifles fire at these
old men in armour with disease
    and rancour scored
so that some nations will increase,
    O Lord, O Lord.

And why is Joshua at the head
of that nocturnal vengeful raid –
on God's obsessive purified
    and jet-black business.
See that red sun in faith divide
    the morning's haziness.

Why is it decorated jets
are blasting at these phantom fêtes?
What terrible and antique debts
    are they collecting?
And who are the neolithic bêtes
    noires they're selecting?

But remember when you drop your bomb
with your mechanical aplomb
it's not a creed that you entomb
    but a human being.
It's not a demon from the womb
    that lies there dying,

but someone made from blood and bones
and not Idea's monotones,
who runs about among these stones
        in nervous fear.
This is his house and this his sons
        and this the dear

locus in which he grew and throve,
this mountain, river, and this grove,
this place with which he fell in love,
        by time endeared.
O simplify both birth and grave.
        Nature's not weird

with phantoms, ghostly parasites.
There are no demons, ghastly lights,
there are no looming Absolutes
        by running streams.
Ideas don't, like prostitutes,
        patrol those glooms

or sunny or brilliant domains.
What animal will send in chains
another animal, through lanes
        of stunning beauty,
or say, 'I must beat out its brains,
        for that's my duty.'

What supertiger ever rose
to cry, 'The zebras and the does,
the lions, elephants, and moose
        must be made extinct.
I had a dream and this I chose
        for mink and lynx.'

Or worse: 'Some tigers don't obey
true tiger laws. And so I say
that they be banned from out our rayed
    and purer species
for they are errant and outré.
    It's not auspicious

'to have them in our pleasing wood
striped with such brilliant sun and shade.
This is the place where we reside –
    Death to those others!
It's time to deal out fratricide
    to our lost brothers!'

What a nightmare if we saw
tiger with tiger, claw with claw,
rip out eye and ear and jaw
    in bloody strife.
'There's one with a minor flaw –
    let's seek its life.'

While eagle against eagle fought
or lark with lark, or stoat with stoat,
or crow with crow till the very light
    was obscenely darkened,
and our beloved and vernal wood
    was thickly blackened

with wings and beaks and claws and teeth,
a seething universe of death,
a snake strikes up with lustrous mouth
    and pliant body.
A crow types out a monograph
    on an unsteady

dying crow, and there a raven,
diving imperiously from heaven,
attacks another while a lion
    joins the red wheel.
And see that whale that's hugely dying
    by another whale.

A cat runs with a dying cat,
a dead rat dangles from a rat,
a mouse clutches a mouse. And what
    is this I see?
A bear is gnawing a bear by that
    great frozen sea.

And nightingales, symbols of our art,
tear at each other's pulsing heart
while sinuous naked worms upstart
    to bite their eyes.
What horrifying à la cartes
    propped undisguised,

against that beech tree or that ash!
Here a stripe and there a gash,
and elsewhere the tremendous lash
    of a python's tail.
Primaeval venomous mish mash
    of tooth and nail.

If this were so, how stunned we'd draw
backwards from such tooth and claw,
and hear the terrible haw haw
    of sarcastic ass
or laughing hyena or jackdaw
    at their black mass.

Tiger chortling on an oak,
lion rocking on a rock,
monkey scratching at his slack
    and greyish stomach,
a crow with his satiric croak
      on a neighbouring hummock.

Such laughter, sarcasm, lampoons.
Cats cavorting in cartoons.
Lizards playing flute-like tunes
    in brilliant green.
The cruel smiles of dingos, coons,
      in nature's scene.

Everything turned tapsalteerie.
The moon, which once was friendly, eerie.
The sun once golden in its glory
    now red as blood.
Pheasant, flamingo, peacock, lory,
      stalking the wood.

But the beasts remain in nature's order
and only man presumes to murder
his fellow man, become the warder
    of the opposition.
From windows men with a last shudder
    jump out of prison

as from the Bible-toting Boers,
whom divine testaments endorse
to bury the black in a black hearse
    since he's inferior
or give him a different address
    post-coded Terror.

Or Indians harried by alcoholic
whites: or apostolic
Spanish priests may bring symbolic
    chalice and pyx
to chase the Incas from idyllic
    streams to the Styx.

Or men sizzling at the stake
so that their bodies may be baked
from sinful flesh for God's good sake
    to a fresh consistent
main course that's tasty, not opaque,
    but lean and pristine

just like the soul no one has seen,
transcendent brilliant window pane,
which men may polish to a green
    or azure hue.
What horrors that transparent screen
    has brought to view!

What massacres accompany
its visitations from the sky,
what pale diaphanous angels fly
    and rest on branches
or like the CIA will spy
    by doors and fences.

O 'soul' how you've been turned and twisted.
How often too you've been arrested
as if you really had existed
    (though beasts of course
don't shine with you but with digested
    and common grass).

O 'soul', invented jewel, how
you have converted spade and plough
to sword and shield: and will allow
    'cleansing' for 'murder'.
I see you bowed with hand on brow,
    a saintly warder.

O your vocabulary's varied.
Assassins promulgate the 'spirit',
'patriot' becomes a 'pirate',
    'stake' becomes 'cross'.
The poets whitening in their garrets
    are your worst foes.

Polish the soul, O keep it bright.
It illuminates the sniper's sight.
It is the brilliant hard light
    interrogators
use as they separate wrong from right,
    good men from traitors.

It is the watch the hangman wears.
It is the driver of the hearse.
It is the fated absolute cause
    that brings the priest.
It is an everlasting force
    to all the blest.

Invisible hypothesis.
Explanatory gloss of glosses.
Among our poor philosophies
    tall apparition
arising above gains and losses,
    transcendent vision.

Impeccable crystal, in your name
what catalogues of grief and shame
have shown a lurid panoram-
    a of obscene photos
horrific gallery and dram-
    a of gaunt ghettoes.

Dissevered heads, dissevered arms,
reveille of confused alarms,
gouged-out eyes, blood-spattered forms,
    O not Platonic,
snake-like undulating worms,
    blind, catatonic.

A theory can saw a leg,
a theory can send a plague,
a theory can make a thug
    into a saint,
a theory can make a rogue
    into a gent.

O, it can burn a house, a neighbour,
or blast a fishing boat from harbour,
enthuse a prison camp with ardour
    of rubbishy books.
And on a green and pleasant arbour
    send down the axe

imperative, huge and keen,
Damoclean or Damascene,
it flashes through the summer scene,
    condign and pure,
supported in its brilliant sheen
    by literature.

O sweep these hills of their divine
angels, devils, crystalline
familiars: and let them shine
        with natural light.
Why turn water into wine,
        day into night,

with witches, wizards, demons, dire
pictures of eternal fire,
'sin' that stalks the innocent shire
        with scarlet dress,
and rises from plain mud and mire
        with sinuous grace.

Let vampires, ghosts, and phantoms die
with horoscopes, astrology,
the second sight, and sorcery
        of dim seances,
voices from a twilight sky,
        conveyances

from some exclusive glimmering planet,
spiritual, infinite,
from which a sort of faint admonit-
        ory finger
points to our earth and all that's on it,
        often with anger.

The sun's engaging shining ring
marries with earth and sky, where sing
the larks and not the seraphim:
        and hawks and eagles
above the hazy waters wing,
        or keep their vigils.

Crocuses and snowdrops brighten
the grass which our own gaze enlightens
and excite our joyful minds to write in
        sunny metres,
or from that canvas a tall painting
        serenely glitters,

from superfluity of delight
or imitation, sparkling wit,
or formal eloquence or obit-
        uary yearning.
And so let men and objects sit
        to art's good morning.

Customs and myths inform the paint,
Mary, angel, child and saint,
messengers divinely sent
        from highest heaven.
In hell some are condignly burnt,
        some are forgiven.

The low mediaeval ceiling rises
to a far airier, more spacious,
sky: and then precocious
        Renaissance man
bestrides the picture, just as Venus
        steps out of sin's

shell, her marvellous hair unbound.
Nature encircles us around.
This is the common natural ground
        in which we flourish
until by natural descent
        we gravely perish.

Though executive business men enwreathed
the skies with smoke. The children breathed
fire and anguish. The unclothed
        were clothed with death.
Thrift and industry were leagued
        with God Himself,

and puritan capitalists upraised
inhuman tenements and praised
God on Sundays. At their breasts
        great watches hung.
Employees became so much waste.
        Children were flung

in furnaces of mediaeval hell.
Where was heaven? They might smell
its rural parishes when will
        finally died
but for the moment iron bells
        insistently cried

and, sold like knick-knacks, among smoke,
they fried and died and choked and broke
so that the huge imperial oak
        might be a mast
on seas of triumph where guns spoke
        to a slaving mass.

And Empire, God, together grew
to redden all that brown and blue,
and priests would follow and construe
        their big black bibles
to equally black inhabitants who
        assigned their troubles

to ignorance of old Isaiah,
the coming of a white Messiah,
the justice of sacrifice and fire
        or exegesis
on Moses, Aaron, Obadiah,
        or infant Jesus.

And slaves from Africa were classed
as subhuman beings, therefore cast
on foreign coasts as so much trash
        shed by the tide
of gold and avarice and cash
        and genocide.

Man's inhumanity to man:
his legacy of grief and pain,
worse than the tiger or the lion,
        constricts the heart
and makes us often 'howling' run
        to our safe art.

Till we remember how it was
that killers would play Berlioz
or enjoy the artificial laws
        of operatic
librettos. God, like Santa Claus,
        solved problematic

tangles of Illyrian love.
O dearest art should not behave
as if the millions who're deceived
        by deceit, chicanery,
should die alone, and unengraved
        by stone or finery.

They cry to us, they weep and wail,
unarmed, unlegged, they face the hail
of snow or bullets, are impaled
    on false ideas
or changed to demons, they exhale
    a fiery fear.

O see Man as he really is
in all his frightened nakedness
not in blue or emerald dress
    or sombre black,
at a terrestrial address,
    terrace or shack.

Imagine him as you yourself
in nature's mirror, the same stuff
as time consumes, both sweet and rough,
    till you descend,
like him, into a natural grave,
    while naïvely-penned

obituaries recall his days
in stray sentence or in phrase,
for these are his 'immortal' bays,
    and not the legend
of 'soul' or other spiritual gloss,
    or glorious pageant.

Who'd not prefer to be recalled
for generosity or mild
behaviour to the human kind
    he daily meets?
Who'd not prefer his tombstone signed
    with his good deeds?

Who'd rather be a cold Augustus,
a merciless medium of justice
or avid intellectual Faustus:
        or merely human
helper, not severe Procrustes
        of tortured foeman.

Who'd rather not when evening comes
turn from the music of the drums
and die with honour in his home's
        decent environs
nor think of harsh imperial Rome
        but with abhorrence.

Who'd rather not remember his
human decisions, sacrifice,
difficult journeys, expertise,
        in work or garden,
than how he cravenly appeased
        a stone-faced Gorgon,

and was enticed by a hot faith
to pour out a discriminate death
on children to whom we should bequeath
        kindness and love
instead of a wild explosive wreath.
        a theory's proof.

And who would see them as he dies –
those socketless, unjewelled eyes,
that buzzing bustle of black flies
        those legless bodies,
and with blind arrogance confess:
        'Those were my studies

'as scholar and experimenter,
chemist, scientist, inventor.
I cut them off from life's adventure
        for "such a reason"
I passed my apprentice's indenture
        in stylish fashion.'

O who would when his day is done
admire the lineaments of a gun,
let cold aesthetic lines condone
        him and his creed,
the hermit zealot without friend
        but his own light.

O Archimedean of terror,
'Eureka' of a blood-stained Marat,
simple replica of a narrow
        sect or tribe,
wearing a sacerdotal aura,
        Druidic robe.

If you should ask me for my heroes,
I'd say that they are the various
artists who have shown in serious
        poem or picture
the human face, or multifarious
        colours of nature.

Burns or Blake, severe Lucretius,
all those who have admired our species
on their auspicious inauspicious
        marvellous journey.
So I'd really rather have Confucius
        than Zeus or any

deus ex machina sent
to untangle a dénouement
or superstitiously invent
    a happy ending,
and subtly alter the account,
    aloof, transcendent.

My poem would be *Ode to Autumn*,
a grave melodious earthly hymn
to who we are and will become
    on this dear earth.
We're found in this continuum,
    and are betrothed

to nature's destiny.
              We're dyed
with nature's livery, reside
in this our home, reamplified
    by art and music
such as this indigenous ode,
    illustrious, classic.

What lovely harmonious music this,
bare and yet mellifluous,
affirmative and luminous.
    Swallows prepare
to set off for another house
    from here to there.

And we inhabit nature too
though on high wings we never flew
but in this scent from green and blue,
    violet, red,
we live, and each of us pursues
    his common trade.

And so we live and so we die.
Like mouse or cat or dog we grow,
like roses that in summer blow
        and later wither
we fall upon the ground below
        as late clouds gather.

And death remains in front of us,
enormous face, conspicuous
barrier, set out in space,
        for, unlike beasts,
we're conscious in advance of this
        ubiquitous west.

And this perhaps is why we write
or paint, compose, before the night
removes from us the daily light,
        that marvellous medium
in which we sculpt or else indite
        plot or exordium.

For death, though natural, may discover
us passionate in diurnal fever
of documents and books and clever
        seething ideas,
and these we have to leave forever
        whatever pleas

we make, or prayers or lonely cries,
whatever metaphor we devise,
whatever proofs we, unrevised,
        may leave on desks.
Word processors unenergised
        with our last discs

stand on the table. Our typewriter,
the long unfinished personal letter,
the comfort of a literature,
        all these must lie
among the daily formless litter,
        No reply

will ever come.
                        And this our car,
our home, our studio, or bar,
possessions common or bizarre,
        we leave behind,
the crossword, dictionary, the far
        horizons of mind.

That lovely garden with its dahlias,
the fragrance of roses or azaleas,
the breeze that mildly will exhale
        from amaryllis,
all these flowers that would avail to us
        a constant solace

will, in brief colour, shine then fade.
The shirt in which we were once arrayed,
the razor and the razor blade:
        and that tall wardrobe
we must bequeath. For we're the dead,
        pardoned, unpardoned,

and we leave behind our wife and child,
the colourful theatre of our wild
or guileless youth. So we're reviled
        or else admired.
We are ourselves our own self-styled
        and final word.

But, too, in nature it occurs
that the rabbit munching common grass
may by the stoat be seized by force,
        or mouse by cat,
or in this huge universe
        a deer is caught

by leaping tiger, leopard, lion,
and no advertisement or sign
will in tall firmament enshrine
        its quick sad going
nor will a star or comet shine
        to mark its dying.

Whether we're the apex, whether not –
surely we are in art and thought –
who on the other hand would rot
        in mindless age?
Rather like natural things let's jot
        no final message

but like the apple or the pear,
a ripple in the atmosphere,
a dappled leaf, a corn's late ear,
        austerely fall,
though in the forest we can hear
        no sound at all.

In such procession take our place,
magnificent, illustrious,
brilliant, unambiguous,
        autumnal colour
our only heaven, only grace,
        success or failure.

Above us is that jewellery,
local moon and local sky,
that no 'divine' astrology
        signs with our names
and whether we live or whether we die
        is all the same

to that indifferent parade.
Nor Romeo nor Juliet,
though they should sparkle in that light,
        is known to it,
or Hamlet's or Othello's great
        speeches or wit,

nor comedy in rustic wood,
nor tragedy of bad or good,
reverberate at that altitude,
        exclusive sphere
far from human bones and blood,
        and our severe

or calm last acts. We're on our own,
and all our choices are homegrown,
and any mortal John or Joan
        is not excused
by horoscope – or is condoned
        by distant Zeus.

So therefore, human as we are,
in this vast theatre, whether 'star'
or extra in its great bazaar's
        dramatis personae
we're equal before nature's bare
        and rich arena.

As human beings, we are so,
beyond whatever dress we glow
in briefly: whether beau
        or tenement dweller.
whether we're Bardot or Monroe
        or Yuri Geller.

Nature's indifferent to our ego.
Against its spacious imago
we're tiny, pitiful and meagre.
        That is the lesson
and the everlasting logos
        that human reason

must learn, for no one can be spared
from death's exuberant – not abhorred –
cupboard. And a ludicrous lord
        is the same to it
as a worker in Nissan or in Ford.
        Since we are set

in nature thus, in such a style,
dependent on each other's skill
an intricate factory or mill,
        a mutual body
that still is individual –
        Flora or Freddy –

which is more important then,
plumber or plasterer or en-
gineer, watchmaker or Gen-
        uine Tailor,
actor, actress, prince or sen-
        atorial

personage in a Parliament.
O let us hope that all consent
to see this transient tenement
    as our best home
and pay our individual rent.
    And though for some

not all is well, yet human kind
by such community entwined
may soon be brought to a refined
    correctness of seeing
and look without being wholly blind
    at the human being.

For as it is, the just, unjust,
the high, the low, may be reversed
and join the endless trails of dust
    of refugees,
the irremediably lost,
    in cold, disease.

And no political idea
on this small diminishing sphere
will save us till we *see*; and hear
    our brother's voice
human and pure and crystal clear
    beyond the noise

of radio, video, TV,
tills and polls and heresy,
the vicious demogoguery
    that fills our days,
the will to power, humbuggery,
    the ego's blaze.

For, as our human globe constricts,
where is the room for tribes and sects,
and terrorists who study texts
    by the bomb's light,
divinely messianic scripts
    that detonate

the globe to a terminal inferno,
not the fictitious, eternal,
hell, but common and diurnal
    terrestrial fire,
and that will be our last corona,
    bouquet and pyre,

our own devisal for this globe,
our own reprisal and hubbub,
and our fine fashioned Nessus robe
    precisely woven
on which we personally inscribe
    a phantom heaven.

'And this dear world I set on flame
for petty flag, for local psalm,
for race or colour or sublime
    command from space;
the visible I set and prime
    by invisible laws.

'For metaphysical design,
for philosophical divine
formulas that make it mine
    and not another's:
I make it gloriously shine
    by inward weathers

'and send the mountains up in smoke,
and make the fearful animals flock
to shelter by that shadowy rock;
        and burn the roses,
daisies, geraniums, to baroque
        metamorphosis.'

Let's put away our childish dolls,
our superstitious fol-de-rols,
and then adapt antique St Paul's
        words in this place;
'We see at first through a crystal ball,
        then face to face.'

But it's the human face we see,
denuded of mythology,
and then the Me becomes the He
        as in a mirror
not devil, demon, enemy.
        Caught in a furor

belli or transcendent evil.
We all must live inside this civil
house that is green or brown.
                        Our novel
        of daily news
is also libretto, or a travel
        book we peruse,

multifarious multi-voiced
as in a novel of James Joyce
so let us eternally rejoice
        in this bright present
where is no virtue or a vice,
        pleasing, unpleasant,

just or unjust, but we make it so.
O why not taste the to and fro
drama of sunlight and of snow,
    theatrical
brilliant, astonishing, show.
    And if we're critical,

create our music and our art,
O not dogmatic but a sort
of praise, or ladder from the heart
    empathic, glorious:
at humanity's multifarious court
    narrate our stories,

our carnivals of joy and grief,
our festivals of love and life,
creative colloquies of stuff
    in words and pictures.
Our life is various enough
    among the creatures,

flowers and landscapes, to rejoice
in operas, scenarios, verse.
There is no old primaeval curse,
    original sin.
Nor is there a black eternal hearse
    to travel in.

But natural harmonies, dissonances,
births and funerals and dances,
the novelty of circumstances
    or their routine,
creative accidents, romances,
    the changing scene

of this our home.
                    This is our heaven,
this is our axiom, the given,
in which forgiving, unforgiving,
        we are the cause:
and we are loving or unloving
        by human laws.

This house we build at any moment
is just our own. Whether it's clement,
inclement, no lineament
        of god excuses,
and nothing in the firmament
        of phantom houses

is model for us, as we go,
ourselves the kings, ourselves the No
or yes of this immense tableau
        we're busy at.
The marvellous roses richly blow,
        and then they fade

as we do also, as we do:
but let's not weep. Let us be true
to one another in these blue
        and green environs,
and say good morning or adieu
        in these bright torrents

of what is always wholly new.
Dearest concurrence!

And let our last affirmative view
be like Rome or Florence.